D1553876

It Doesn't Have to Be This Way

Common Sense Essentials for Raising Great Catholic Kids and Bringing Peace to Your Home

by Ginny Seuffert

vseuffert@sbcglobal.net

Printed in the United States of America.

ISBN: 978-1-60704-124-5

Published by Seton Press.
Visit us on the Web at http://www.setonbooks.com/

SETON PRESS
1350 Progress Drive
Front Royal, VA 22630

Table of Contents

Note Before You Start Reading

In my experience, children seem to fall into one of three categories. Some just seem easy right from birth. They sleep the night at an early age, do not care if their schedules are disrupted, rarely raise a fuss about anything, and are generally cheerful and cooperative. Let's just call them "Easy Kids." At the opposite side of the spectrum, some children are difficult from the start. These are the ones who cry at the drop of a hat, throw tantrums when they do not get their way, refuse to eat what is put in front of them, cannot tolerate any change of routine, and turn the simplest request into a battle of wills. Sometimes referred to as strong-willed, we'll call these kids the "Challengers" because they challenge even the best of parents. The large majority of children, however, fall somewhere in the middle. These Middle Majority Children present challenges from time to time, respond well to competent parenting, and can be swayed in either direction by good or poor influences in their lives.

Parents of Middle Majority Children will find this book offers some useful advice. Middle Majority Children will benefit from calm, confident parenting that encourages them to develop Christian virtues, so over time parental controls are replaced by self-control. Personal discipline will become their shield against the bad influences of modern American living. Moms of Easy Kids have been known to remark that their offspring could be "raised by wolves" and still turn out fine, but even these children may occasionally lie or show their tempers. Easy Kid parents might want to stow this book on a shelf and pull it out for some ideas on those occasions when Junior seems to be straying off the path just a bit. Even the best-behaved children require an occasional correction, but mostly these parents should just continue doing what they already do. It seems to be working just fine.

Common Sense Essentials for Raising Great Catholic Kids is especially directed to parents of Challengers. Home life is not peaceful, and your children often embarrass you in public by their outbursts and unruly conduct. Try as you will, you cannot seem to find the proper mix of encouragement and consequences to make meaningful change. You feel helpless and often go to sleep exhausted by the battles that begin at breakfast and continue until bedtime. Keep this book close at hand. My own experience shows me that the following ideas will prove enormously helpful to you. I assure you that, given a bit of time, and coupled with prayer, consistent, calm, confident parenting does work. It is up to the test of raising even the toughest Challenger.

Please remember that the author of *Common Sense Essentials for Raising Great Catholic Kids* is not a pediatrician or a Ph.D. This book is intended to help parents by presenting some ideas that work but does not pretend to address problems of children with unique medical or mental health needs. It is certainly not a substitute for a pediatrician. I base my ideas on forty years of experience as a mother of twelve and, as of this writing, grandmother of eighteen. Their father and I are proud of the educational and professional accomplishments of our children, but the love they have for God, the Catholic Church, their parents, and one another is our greatest achievement. Common sense essentials worked for us; they can work for you too.

Introduction

Behavior on the Brain

For over twenty years, I have been counseling mothers and fathers who are either homeschooling or seriously considering the idea. With years of experience under my belt, I am able to help them set up their school days, pick educational materials, and even keep their houses neat and tidy. What I *cannot* do is make their children obey them. This is a problem as it can be pretty tough teaching the ABC's to children when they are racing around the desk, instead of sitting at it.

No question, discipline, or rather its lack, is the number one challenge facing homeschooling families. In my experience, it is the primary reason parents hesitate to begin home education, "What will I do if the kids don't listen to me?" It is a very common motivation parents have to cease homeschooling and put their children back in institutional school. "I was spending my days yelling and screaming. That's not how I want my children to remember their school years—or their mother." Interestingly, the lack of discipline in brick and mortar schools is also a common motivation for parents to undertake home education in the first place. "My son's teacher was spending so much time dealing with uncontrollable, wild kids that she was ignoring the serious students who actually wanted to learn."

With all the thoughts, words, and actions directed towards discipline in the United States, one would think we would have more of it!

Kids out of Control

This conversation about out-of-control children is certainly not limited to the home education community. Pass by any playground and you will hear children whining and wailing while their caregivers try, and often fail, to reason with them. Restaurant patrons routinely ask not to be seated next to families with children, so they can actually enjoy their meals, free from flying food and blubbering babies. At our local public library, my daughter observed one boy, who appeared to be five or six years old, rolling around on the floor for at least ten minutes, crying, kicking, and shouting. What brought on such a violent tantrum? He had to share a play area with other children.

Children with special emotional and behavioral needs are overwhelming our schools, forcing them to fund a variety of expensive interventions including teacher aides in classrooms, social workers, and school psychologists. In 2008, 2.8 million students in U.S. schools were being treated with prescription medication for Attention Deficit Disorder, a condition that virtually everyone believes is over-diagnosed with the intent of controlling misbehavior with drugs. Parents feel stressed and helpless, fueling an entire industry of magazine articles, books, videos, and parenting classes. Even reality TV has jumped on board with shows like *Supernanny* and *Nanny 911*. Tellingly, although I leave little doubt about my socially conservative and observant Catholic worldview, more than one couple has told me that they have surgically guaranteed they will never have another child because they simply "cannot handle" the ones they already have.

Does it have to be like this?

No!

There were sixty six-year-olds—that's right, sixty!—in my first grade class at St. John the Baptist School in Yonkers, a few blocks north of the New York City border. Sixty kids, one nun with no aide, and you could have heard a pin drop. We all sat in our seats, remained silent, rose only to answer questions, but automatically jumped to our feet when an adult entered the classroom. Students only addressed Sister by name, paid attention, and exclusively used #3 pencils, as Sister frowned on the messy work produced by #2 pencils. Mine was not an isolated case; my husband Ed had a similar experience some miles away in Brooklyn. In fact, speak to any Catholic grade school alumnus from the early and mid-twentieth century and the report will be virtually identical.

Nor is this some quaint reminiscence from a different era. Children from other nations and cultures routinely behave well, study hard, and assume responsibilities considered extraordinary for their age by modern American standards. Nor are these children miserable and mistreated. In fact, when judged on a crying, whining, and wailing scale, well-disciplined children seem considerably happier than their brattier counterparts.

So what happened?

Some of the blame can be laid on the doorstep of the changes in society that occurred in the last four decades of the twentieth century. Common, widely shared Judeo-Christian moral principles were called into question, leaving parents confused about the right way to form their children's character, or even if they should try to form it at all. As society became more mobile, young families moved away from the extended family, leaving behind the wisdom of an older, wiser generation. For guidance, young parents substituted talk show hosts and articles they read in magazines picked up at the supermarket checkout line. Their parental philosophy was often copied from the most convincing, or even most recent, book they read on the topic.

Dr. Ray Guarendi is a Catholic clinical psychologist, author, talk show host, and popular lecturer. He believes that for the past several decades, it is the poor advice of so-called child-rearing professionals that has watered down discipline. Parents have been urged to enforce rules with a mixture of logic, persuasion, communication, rewards, and guidance. This has not worked, claims Dr. Ray, because it "isn't clear-cut, firm, and enforced at the hand of a confident parent."

Can anything be done?

Of course! And it does not have to take years of painful adjustment.

My daughter Carol took a crowd of children on an outing one sunny day to give their moms a break. The children shouted, pushed, and shoved as they ran towards the van, and confusion reigned as she tried to get them to buckle in. Carol, perhaps regretting her generosity, looked at me anxiously. "Was this what it was like for you to take all of us out for the day?"

I did not want to insult the nearby mothers, so I just quietly responded, "No. No, that was not the way it was."

Driving to the park, Carol remembered day trip rules from her childhood, and laid down the law. No loud voices, pushing, or shoving. Older children were assigned a younger buddy, and everyone had to line up by twos and hold hands when walking in the parking lot. Once clear guidelines were established in a no-nonsense way, the children were terrific, and everyone, including Carol, enjoyed the day.

Help is on the way!

I had twelve children and would have been happy to have twelve more. I loved being a parent. It was hard work, and I certainly had some moments when my children frustrated or disappointed me, but most of the time I enjoyed our time spent together. I admit to being extraordinarily proud of the adults they have become.

Many parenting styles enjoy popularity today: attachment parenting, positive parenting, tiger mom parenting, slow parenting, helicopter parenting, free-range parenting, the list goes on and on. Each of these, while often wildly contradictory, contains some grains of truth, so where is a parent to turn? The ideas in this book are simple, common sense, tried-and-true techniques that have worked for centuries. They are based on my own experience, and that of other mothers and fathers, and a few professionals, who have observed what it takes to raise well-behaved children who become adults with unwavering Christian character and impeccable integrity. You might call it "straightforward" or "common sense" parenting.

Despite what you may have read, raising good kids is not a complicated process requiring family meetings and performance charts. It is hard work and asks that parents be a bit counter-cultural, but superior parenting is mostly common sense. Busy parents do not have much spare time, so this book is intentionally short and to the point. It is directed to Catholic parents who are educating their children at home, but any parent can put these techniques into practice.

Get started today!

Chapter 1

Establish Authority

Honor your father and your mother, that you may have a long life in the land which the Lord, your God, is giving you.

- Exodus 20:12

Some years ago, I taught the Confirmation class for our parish religious education program. The class was never rowdy or rude; my students were attentive and engaged – a pleasure to teach. A lovely lady from the parish volunteered to substitute when I was away one weekend. The following week, she told me the class had misbehaved so terribly that they had reduced her to tears. To tears! I was horrified and insisted each student apologize individually to her, but I was also quite surprised. What had turned my model students into monster brats? The answer was NOT that I exercised better control over the class; I didn't feel that I had to control them at all. They just seemed to mind me.

My "secret" was that, from the very first moments, I had established my clear authority over the class. Using confident body language, a firm and friendly tone, and a no-nonsense attitude, I let them know, right from the start, that I was in charge. The students and I had an unspoken agreement, that I would provide them with what they needed to be confirmed, and they in turn would pay courteous attention. That being settled, we could all enjoy our time together – and we did. The same principle applies to family life. Mom and Dad lovingly, but firmly, set the rules and the kids obey. Once that is understood and accepted, we can eliminate begging, whining, crying, arguing, yelling – well, mostly eliminate them – and family life becomes a pleasure.

A National Emergency

It is certainly no secret that American parents (taken as a whole; there are some lovely exceptions) have not accepted their own authority over their children. As a result, instead of enjoying family life, they find childcare a stressful burden, and home life an endless round of begging, pleading, ignoring, cajoling, and hollering in an effort to make their children behave. In our nation's public schools, educational journals claim that as much as half of a teacher's time is spent in "classroom management," thus wasting the taxpayers' money and robbing better-behaved students of the education they deserve. In public, loud bratty children often turn dining out, shopping, or even a trip to the library, church, or park, into a major headache for parents and innocent bystanders. No one, not even a person with no children, is safe from public tantrums. Out-of-control kids are fast becoming the problem of every citizen.

The American Way?

We Americans value independence and autonomy as virtues, and hope our children will grow up to value them as well. For decades, child professionals have warned us that strong discipline and authoritative parents risk turning children into fearful little robots who will lack self-esteem, initiative, and imagination. Experts advise us not to inflict our own will on our kids, but to let them make their own choices. Misbehavior is simply a step in the growing-up process, a sign of immaturity that will be somehow magically resolved by the passage of time.

Actually, misbehavior is an opportunity for parents to establish their own authority and then use that authority to inculcate better patterns of conduct. In other words, parents take their longer life experience, their better judgment, their more developed sense of right and wrong, and the high expectations they hold for their children, and then they teach them virtuous right living. The key is not to form the children's will to robotically obey their parents. Rather it is to form their hearts and minds so they do the right thing, on their own, with less and less direction from their mothers and fathers, as the years go by.

Wisdom of the Ages

The wisdom of the ages, as well as our own good common sense, tells us this is the path to follow. Our great-grandmothers would have scratched their heads in bewilderment had we asked them if our children should respect and obey us. Although often lacking the benefits of a formal education, our ancestors knew it was not the role of parents to provide children with momentary happiness —or themselves with momentary peace—by satisfying every demand. They accepted that during childhood parents had the responsibility, even the sacred obligation, to teach their children a host of virtues beginning with obedience and respect. As children grew and matured, they inculcated courtesy, industriousness, honesty, sincerity, purity, modesty, humility, selflessness, resourcefulness, and many more good habits of life. Our forebears knew that upright living was the source of a happy and productive life here on Earth, and eternal joy in Heaven. Parents understood that virtuous children are a joy to bring up, a source of gratification when they reach adulthood, and a comfort to their parents during their final years. I suspect our forebears often meditated on the Proverb, "A wise son makes his father glad, but a foolish son is a grief to his mother" (Prov. 10:1).

God's Will for His People

This proverb is still true and is confirmed by Judeo-Christian doctrine and tradition. "Honor thy father and thy mother" is the first of the Commandments that regulate how God's people are to treat one another. So important were well-ordered families to Hebrew life that the Law of Moses ordered that, "Whoever curses his father or mother shall be put to death" (Ex. 21:17). God tells the Israelites to "Revere your mother and father" (Lev. 19:3). Parents have the obligation to instruct their children. "Raise up a child in the way he should go; even when he is old, he will not depart from it" (Prov. 22:6). Children have the responsibility to obey. "Hear, my son, your father's instructions, and reject not your mother's teachings" (Prov. 1:8). In his letter to the Colossians, St. Paul confirms this teaching for the early Christians: "Children, obey your parents in all things, for that is pleasing to the Lord" (Col. 3:20).

Mothers and fathers can assume their rightful authority over their children in the confident knowledge that Catholic teaching requires it and the experience of generations of parents confirms it. Everyday family life becomes more peaceful and serene, as children are a joy, not a burden. Best of all, parents are preparing their children to be responsible citizens in this world and saints in the next.

Chapter 2

Start Strong! Win the Food War.

*A crust eaten in peace is better than a
banquet partaken in anxiety.*

- Aesop

An American living in France, Pamela Druckerman, shared the mortification so many parents experience when eating in public. Her toddler daughter, nicknamed "Bean," gave her parents a narrow window of opportunity in restaurants before she began to throw food and scramble to run around. Her finicky diet consisted of pasta, French fries, and baguettes. Druckerman and her husband were even more embarrassed when they compared Bean's antics to native French toddlers who sat patiently in their seats, waiting for their meals, and then contentedly munched on whatever was served, including vegetables. What was the secret of French parenting? In her book *Bringing Up Bébé*, she shares her observations about the French customs that produce happy little gourmets, and she shows that even very young children can be taught to do the right thing.

Any place on the globe, an effective parent is one who gives good example, corrects early and often, and is calm, confident, and consistent. Loving correction builds good habits—another name for virtues—in children, so the need for discipline will lessen over time. Moreover, by insisting that your children do the correct thing, in this case eating what is put in front of them, babies learn they cannot inflict their own will, but must obey. Newborn babies need to have their basic needs (eating, comfort, and a diaper change) met when the demand arises, but even at an early age, you can be teaching important life skills. Teaching children to approach nutrition obediently, calmly, and patiently will give them a tremendous advantage in life.

Work on Establishing a Feeding Schedule

Virtually every medical association concerned with maternal and infant health recommends exclusively breastfeeding for baby's first six months of life, unless there are medical indications to the contrary. Nursing infants are fed on demand, but as the weeks go by, some mothers encourage baby to feed for longer periods of time at each session. The aim is to fill up baby's tummy, leaving more time between feedings. Every baby responds differently to this strategy; some of my own would just not go along with Mom's plan. When it works, however, a full tummy discourages baby from "snacking" every hour or so, which leads to a constantly needy baby and an exhausted mother. Keep nursing on demand, but remember that babies can be comforted by something other than a feeding. If baby just ate, try walking around, or speaking calmly, or in some other way distracting her from her demand to nurse constantly.

When baby is ready for solid food, try to introduce it on a schedule. For example, many mothers who are anxious for baby to sleep the night give first solids at supper, hoping a full belly will translate into a full night of sleep. When that is well tolerated, add solids to breakfast and lunch, perhaps nursing in between. By his or her first birthday, your toddler should be eating solids on a schedule similar to this one: breakfast at 7:30 A.M.; snack at 10 A.M.; noon lunch; snack at 3 P.M.; supper at 6 P.M. Breastfeeding continues on demand.

With a regular predictable schedule, baby learns patience waiting, but is happy because he can depend on his meals coming on time. Mom is happier because she is not constantly preparing snacks or cleaning the kitchen. Because meals and snacks are planned, baby will be eating healthier. Everyone wins.

Cure for the Finicky Eater

Today many moms are preparing two meals, one for parents and older children, and another one for the little kids. Mom and Dad eat a balanced diet while the kiddies eat off the at-home "children's menu" of chicken tenders, hot dogs, fries, pizza, and frozen waffles. Besides the extra work that double-duty meal prep causes Mom or Dad, this practice has horrible implications for the health of children. Presently one-third of U.S. children are overweight or obese. Type 2 diabetes, formerly seen only in adults over forty, is now being diagnosed in school age children.

Picky eating leads to other problems, not related to health. These kids and their parents are often placed in socially awkward positions when children turn their noses up at food outside the home. They limit the number of restaurants their parents can patronize and the number of homes they can visit. They often turn suppertime into a nightmare.

Every parent realizes that chicken tenders and frozen fries are not a healthy substitute for broiled chicken breast with mixed vegetables and wild rice. Parents of finicky eaters know the downside but, "What can we do?" they ask, "The kids won't eat anything else."

Sure they will! Here's how.

Start off on the Right Foot

Follow your pediatrician's advice, but most babies start solids at about six months old. At the beginning, babies and toddlers seem more open to trying new tastes including pureed veggies, fruits, and meats. Even when they resist, try to present a variety of foods again and again, perhaps mixing some applesauce with the pureed green beans to make them more palatable. Typically as they get older and become more vocal, toddlers complain or turn up their noses at certain tastes and textures. Mom fries up a hot dog, and *voila!* a finicky eater is born. Resist the urge to provide a separate menu for little ones, and half the battle is won. Here are some other ideas:

- Keep to your food schedule. Hungry children are more likely to try something they are not sure about. Children who know they can load up later on cheese puffs have no incentive to finish what's on their plates.

- When your doctor gives the okay, present the same food to your child that everyone else is eating – just chopped or mashed to allow for toothless gums.

- If the baby resists one item from the meal, let him eat more of another selection, but do not prepare anything different.

- Present food that your toddler resists again and again. For example, if baby does not like carrot sticks, try offering them with salad dressing, or cooked or shredded or glazed. Sometimes it takes many tries before a child accepts a new taste or texture.

- As much as possible, refrain from offering the same items typically found on a children's menu: hot dogs, frozen pizza, chicken tenders, and packaged macaroni and cheese. Kids quickly get a taste for these high-fat, high-salt foods and resist anything else.

Is it too late for us?

Some of you may wish you had heard this advice a bit earlier. Your picky eater is six or seven or even ten years old and will only eat a few limited items, none of them very healthy. You keep hoping she will grow out of it. Can anything be done? Of course!

- Be very strict about maintaining your food schedule. Absolutely NO FOOD outside of regularly scheduled meals and snacks. Make sure snacks consist of much less food than an actual meal. Remember, hungry children are more likely to try something new. Five meals/snacks per day are plenty!

- Start with one meal at a time, perhaps supper.

- Offer an "appetizer" tray with healthy foods you want to introduce like cut up fruit or vegetables. Give just a small portion that kids are more likely to taste if they are really hungry.

- Offer variations on favorite foods. For example, if pizza is a usual winner, offer chicken with tomato sauce and cheese. Add pasta. If the kids like fries, try mashed potatoes, or baked, or sweet potato fries.

- Do not turn mealtime into a misery by insisting that the child finish everything on her plate. My generation still has nightmares about gagging down cold, coagulated food.

- Do insist that the child taste a little bit of everything, just two green beans or a tablespoon of corn. Let her eat more of the foods she likes, if any.

- Don't worry if she only eats after picking out every microscopic piece of onion, or smothering it with ketchup. At least she is eating a wide variety, and her taste will improve over time.

- If she refuses to eat anything at all, do not make a big deal of it. Just say, "Okay, but there is nothing else for you. You'll eat a good breakfast tomorrow morning." *And stick to your word.* If you let her have just a few cheesy goldfish outside of the schedule, you have admitted defeat. You want her to be hungry at the next scheduled meal or snack.

You can do it!

The United States is the country that invented the kids' menu. Its negative consequences to health and happiness are obvious. As I grew up before convenience food was so common, my age mates and I ate whatever everyone else at the table ate. In most parts of the world, children eat the same food as adults, and in many places that means they exist on a diet of vegetables and whole grains. There is no reason your children cannot eat whatever is put in front of them.

Some of the suggestions in this chapter may seem a bit harsh to today's parents, but quite the contrary is true. By helping your child conquer his picky taste for food, not only will his health improve, but he will also learn obedience, gain more confidence in social situations, and grow in self-control.

Chapter 3

Bedtime

When you lie down, you need not be afraid; when you rest, your sleep will be sweet.

- Proverbs 3:24

One mom appears to the outside world to be a model homeschooling parent. Her children are academically advanced, win awards for their many accomplishments, and go on to prestigious college programs. Why then does she tell other mothers, "Don't homeschool! I hate my life. I feel as though my kids are holding me hostage!"?

I discovered what might be the source of her frustration one evening when I dropped something off at her house. Although it was pretty late, her children, including toddlers, were still running around. When I remarked, "Wow! Late bedtime tonight," she answered, "Oh, they don't have any particular bedtime. They just sort of run around until they get tired, and then we carry them up."

That explains it all! How can any mom and dad, much less parents of a big family, enjoy life without a break from the kids? No matter how well behaved little ones may be, there simply comes a time when mothers and fathers need to be alone and vaguely remember why they got married in the first place. By a happy coincidence, little children need lots of sleep to achieve optimum health. Before the teen years, children need eleven or twelve hours each night, and even teenagers still need eight or nine hours. By what seems like a Divine Plan, early bedtimes are best for everyone.

Establish a Routine

Children do not understand the clear benefits of a good night's sleep, so it is up to their parents to introduce them to it. As with so many other activities, start with a set schedule and routine as soon as they are able to understand, and maybe even before. If you set 8 P.M. as a bedtime, then start at 7:30. Try to proceed in the same order every night. First, make a stop in the bathroom for a tub or sponge bath and teeth brushing. Insist that the children use the toilet, even if they claim they do not need to. This eliminates a later trip after lights out. Make sure the children stow their own dirty clothing in a hamper, and then get into pajamas. After that, say prayers, perhaps read a story or sing a lullaby, give kisses, and then it's lights out.

This routine may be upset for a while when Junior first learns how to climb out of the crib. Then bedtime may become a battle of wills. Either Mom or Dad has to stay in the room, perhaps reading a book using the light from the hall, and keep putting Junior back into bed, no discussion allowed. You can sweeten the pot with a nightlight or soft music, but he must stay in bed. Don't argue and don't explain. Just stand firm. After a while Junior catches on that all resistance is futile and goes to sleep without an argument.

"I wish someone had told me this when my children were little! Now they're 8 and 10."

It's not too late. Make an announcement. "You children are just not getting up with the energy you need to meet your day. From now on, 8:00 is bedtime. Lights out at 8 P.M."

You do not have to accompany them to the bathroom but do tell them at 7:30 that it is time to get ready. The same routine applies: wash up, change, stow dirty clothing, and say prayers. They can read until 8, and then lights out.

If you have not established a clear line in the past, they might give you a hard time, but persist. Use the same technique as for the little children. Park yourself with a book or your rosary near the bedroom. If he gets out of bed, put him back with no explanation or discussion. With a really strong-willed child, you might have to do this dozens of times the first few nights, but eventually he will catch on. Mom and Dad mean business; they are not giving in.

What about teens?

Teens obviously do not need as much sleep as toddlers. On the other hand, you might need just as many hours of freedom from them, so make a deal. Teens and pre-teens need to go to their rooms at say 8:30, but they can read or do homework. Siblings may play a game quietly together. At the first argument, loud talking, or horsing around Mom or Dad hears, lights go out. If you have already established good sleep patterns, this will not be an issue. I rarely said anything to my older children regarding bedtime. Again, the whole idea of discipline is to raise children who do the right thing without being told.

Naptimes

Before my children hit school age, I was a strict naptime enforcer. Every day after lunch, babies and toddlers went down for a nap. They were so accustomed to this practice that they developed a conditioned response, like Pavlov's dogs. As they chewed on the last few bites of their peanut butter and jelly sandwiches, their little eyelids would start to droop. Any screaming after being placed in the crib was short-lived as they drifted off to sleep. Before the age of three, most would nap for a good two hours each day.

Parents often tell me that their child "gave up" his nap at 18 months. Of course, they admit that the poor little guy's head is on his highchair tray halfway through dinner. Allowing such a late snooze will definitely spoil a good night's sleep. Often, children do not "decide" to give up their naps; they just wear their parents down. If your child is nap-resistant at any early age, this might be a time for some quiet TV or an audiotape. No matter what, Junior must stay in bed (or on the couch, wherever) for at least an hour. Set a timer if you like, and say, "You may not get up until you hear the buzzer." Even the most resistant will usually doze off. Stick to your guns; it's worth it!

A solid nap schedule is invaluable to a homeschooling mother of multiple students. Naptime is when you can get some really uninterrupted time to work on subjects that require concentrated one on one, perhaps an English composition or a book report.

I have been urging homeschooling parents for years to stick to their guns regarding bedtime and naptime. I spoke to a small support group about just this topic, and one woman commented, "I heard you speak about this last year. My children were terrible about sleeping, and my husband and I seemed always grouchy. We stuck to our guns, just like you told us to. It changed our lives!"

Chapter 4

Courtesy

*Speaking evil of none, not quarrelsome but moderate,
showing all mildness to all men.*

- Titus 3:2

Years ago, my eldest son—who now has ten children of his own—attended a military academy near our home. Gabe was a day student, but most of his classmates were boarders, so our house became a popular weekend destination. The cadets were not allowed to keep civilian clothes at school, so they would arrive at our house in uniform, and displayed simply lovely military manners. Even the plainest of meals brought, "Thank you, Ma'am; that was delicious."

When my husband came home from work, our visitors would immediately hop to their feet, shake his hand, and say, "Thanks for having us, Sir. We appreciate the hospitality."

I recall being charmed at the time, and thinking that these manners would take them far in life. Since then, I worked in human resources, and can assure you that the job applicant who greets the interviewer with a firm handshake, sits straight, speaks politely, and sends a thank you note, certainly has a leg up for the job.

Although there are many practical benefits as well, the reason we should practice courtesy is because it is, at heart, a Catholic virtue. The word comes to us from the Old French, spoken in the royal courts of England, which were governed by Christian principles. To be courteous means to act in a noble manner. Courtesy is recognition that each person with whom we come in contact is a child of God made in His image and likeness. Teaching and insisting on Catholic good manners not only makes family life far more pleasant, but it also offers several benefits to your children as well.

- Good manners reinforce the Judeo-Christian view of the intrinsic value of every human being.
- Acting politely instills recognition that other people have needs too. Getting beyond one's own selfish desires is an important step in gaining maturity.
- Courtesy keeps the rambunctious child in check.
- The shy child gets a roadmap of how to interact with others, something that does not come naturally to some.
- Others will treat your children more kindly when they see how respectful they are.
- Everyday family life becomes less stressful when family members interact in a thoughtful and gentle fashion.

- Courtesy is an important and necessary skill for future academic and professional success.
- Children grow in self-control when they act the way common civility dictates instead of being guided by feelings of the moment.

The Guiding Principle

Obviously the first step to instilling good manners is to constantly teach and reinforce the Golden Rule. Our Blessed Lord said, "Therefore all that you wish men to do to you, even so do you also to them; for this is the law and the prophets" (Matt. 7:12). Even toddlers understand, "Would you like it if Andy took your cookie? Don't do that again." Here are some other important markers of a courteous child.

Greeting others with respect

If everyone with whom we come in contact is a child of God, made in His image and worthy of respect, then we must teach little ones to treat each person with proper dignity. The first step is to greet both adults and other children suitably. There are two parts to a polite greeting: first, the actual phrase, and second, the title and name. Phrases include "Hi" or "Hello" for the youngest children, but should quickly progress to "Good morning" or "Good evening." The title is either the person's actual name, "Mrs. Smith," or some polite honorific, such as "Ma'am" or "Sir." School age children are perfectly capable of saying, "Good morning, Mrs. Smith," if they have been prompted to do so during toddler years.

When I was a child growing up in New York, it was unthinkable to call an adult by his or her first name. Even adults we saw on a daily basis and were quite close to remained Mr. or Mrs. Smith. Very close family friends were sometimes called "Aunt" or "Uncle." I always insisted that my own children do the same, as did my neighbors, and I still consider it appropriate. The custom in some parts of the country is to refer to adults as Miz Jeannie or Mr. Pete, which I think is just fine. It just seems more respectful when children do not speak to adults the same way they do to their friends.

Of course, good-bye is as important as hello. Children should never leave the house, or even the room, without some polite farewell like "See you later," "I'll be back at 5," or simply, "Good-bye."

Please and Thank You

Please and thank you are often the first words we teach to our children to instill courtesy. The epitaph on my tombstone should read, "Yes, please, or no, thank you," as I have prompted children using those words probably tens of thousands of times. As soon as they can talk, children must learn never to say, "I want a drink." Each time, they must be corrected, "May I please have a drink," or prompted, "How do you ask?" before receiving anything.

Gratitude is a very attractive habit, and it should be insisted on as early as possible. Always prompt children to say "Thank-you" when anyone gives them anything or does something for them. Every time! Insist that after a day of play or a party away from home, they always thank the host for having them.

Although in a pinch a phone call or email will do, a thank you note is always correct. Many people struggle writing them, but allow Ginny, Mistress of the Correct Note, to give you the formula that works in every situation right up to their wedding gifts. Here is the formula: greeting, direct thank you, nice thought, repeat thanks. That's it. Let me give you an example:

Dear Aunt Jane and Uncle Oscar,

Thank you so much for sending me ten dollars for my birthday. It was such a generous amount that I saved half and used the other half to buy ice cream. Again, thanks so much.

Your niece,

Mary Teresa

Short, sweet, to the point, and it gets the job done.

Just a Bit of Dignity at Dinner

Not too long ago, children were subject to a whole host of rules at the dinner table. While eating quietly, with elbows off the table, and the non-working hand on his lap, a child might speak only when spoken to. While this all may seem just a bit stuffy to today's parents, mealtimes were certainly more pleasant, and there are a few practical rules that still make sense.

- No one eats before grace is said.
- Food and utensils are passed, not reached for.

- Conversation is limited to pleasant, wholesome topics.
- The cook is complimented, never criticized.
- Everyone helps with clean up.

It should go without saying that we chew with our mouths closed, and refrain from doing anything, or making any noise, that would ruin the appetite of others.

Don't Interrupt

A great frustration suffered by most moms is attempting to put a thought into words, while a child is whining, "Mom, Mom, Mom, Mom…" It is rude to interrupt another person's conversation, even if that person is your parent. When I heard, "Mom, Mom, Mom…" I used to say, "Do not dare interrupt unless you are bleeding!"

"Excuse me, Mom. Excuse me, Mom. Excuse me, Mom," is only slightly better. Here are some general rules to instill in your children:

- Never interrupt adult conversation, including phone conversation, for less than an emergency – like someone is hurt. Handle the problem yourself if you can.
- If you absolutely, positively must interrupt, wait for a lull in the conversation.
- Always apologize for interrupting.
- Ask quickly and go about your business.

Teach your children the basic manners of polite society. It will make your home life more pleasant and your school day more productive, and it will prepare them for entrance into society.

Chapter 5

Perfect in the Pew

If you don't behave as you believe, you will end by believing as you behave.

- Venerable Fulton J. Sheen

Many Catholic parents are caught in a major conflict regarding Church attendance. On one hand, they fantasize about well-scrubbed, perfectly-behaved children sitting in the front pew paying close attention during Mass. The reality, however, can be a bit different. Dad stands in the back trying to keep the baby quiet, Mom picks up cheerios that the toddler keeps dropping on the floor, and the older children run back and forth to the rest room. No one, including stressed-out Mom and Dad, actually pays attention to Mass. Must it be like this?

Of course not! Although very young children, under two-years-old, may lack the capacity to sit still, children older than that can be taught to sit quietly, and do much more. Here are a few ideas.

The Under-Two Set

Tiny infants are often a pleasure to take to Mass. They sleep quietly, or nurse discreetly, and Mom and Dad can actually pay attention. In just a few months, though, they become louder and more mobile, but are still too young to understand concepts like "sit still" or "use your inside voice." Some can be distracted with a small toy or treat, but many simply cannot. Parents have two options: first, take trips to the cry room or vestibule, or second, go to Mass in shifts. Although I have twelve children, I can count on one hand the number of Masses I spent in the cry room. My husband and I chose the "shift" option. We both felt that it is a really bad habit to bring a toddler to the pew, anticipating that he will act up, and then "reward" him by allowing him to play with a toy truck in the cry room. On the other hand, we always lived pretty close to a church. We might have chosen the other option if we lived thirty minutes from the nearest Sunday Mass.

Baby Boot Camp

By her second birthday, baby speaks a little, or even quite well, and most likely understands most of what you say. Now is the time to teach her how to behave during Mass, and ironically, the easiest way to start is often not during Mass itself. Take toddlers to church when it is empty. (If your church is usually locked, ask for a key at the rectory. Chances are if the pastor knows you, he will be happy to oblige.) Practice blessing yourselves with holy water, and genuflecting in front of the Blessed Sacrament; toddlers love different gestures and postures. Point out the Tabernacle and explain that Jesus is in there, so we have to be especially good. Show your children statues, stained glass windows, the murals, the stations, and anything else you can think of. Once they understand some of the stories these holy items represent, little children are more likely to occupy themselves during Mass by looking at them.

While I think it can be a good idea to bring books for two- and three-year-olds, try to make them kiddie prayer books or Bible stories with lots of colorful pictures. Consider limiting toys to Noah's Ark animals or perhaps a plastic statue of St. Joseph. Now, this may seem unnecessarily picky to some parents, but I believe that it is important to stress, at a very early age, that church is different from other places. We dress up and speak in hushed voices, or better yet, not at all. We do not run, but we do sit, stand, and kneel when everyone else does. We speak, in our hearts, to Jesus and the Blessed Mother. At all times, our thoughts are on holy people and things.

By four years of age, the majority of children are capable of at least sitting still and not disturbing others during Sunday Mass. Those who are lagging behind obviously need to practice this skill at home. My husband and I found that if we had wiggly children sit in a "quiet practice chair" at home after Mass, behavior improved the following week.

Peaceful Worship at Any Age

A church in my town had a bulletin announcement that read something like this: "*The parish finance committee, after careful study, has decided that it is not presently feasible to build a swimming pool in the main church. Therefore, worshipers who have been coming to Church in pool clothing may now stop doing so."*

Tongue in cheek, sure, but the parish is trying to get a handle on the tank tops, mini skirts, shorts, and flip flops worn to the typical Catholic church in summer. If they have any success with that, they might then move on to people who check email on their phones, and chat loudly before and after Mass. Adults behaving badly give poor example to children who play with toys long past toddler years, munch on pretzels, and leave their pews to use the restroom repeatedly. With all this distraction, it can be tough for motivated parents to get their children to behave appropriately in church – tough but not impossible.

If you have trained your toddlers properly, by the time they are in first grade, they know to be silent when they enter the main part of the church. They genuflect towards the Blessed Sacrament as they enter the pew and then kneel immediately to pray. They sit, stand, or kneel with the congregation. They have memorized the common responses and say them loud enough to be heard. They do not bolt out of the pew after Mass, but remain a few moments in thanksgiving.

I must admit that I had a sneaking suspicion that when my children and I remained after Mass, often not a lot of thanks were being given. To remedy this situation, we would pray quietly together the *Hail Holy Queen*, the *Prayer to St. Michael the Archangel,* and then repeat three times: *Most Sacred Heart of Jesus, have mercy on us.*

For Goodness' Sake, Dress Up!

One simple trick to improve behavior at Mass is to insist that every family member wear "Sunday best." Dressing well helps children understand that Mass attendance is the central event of their lives, and sets the tone for behavior. There are three characteristics of proper church attire. First, it should be modest. It should go without saying that we should cover up before we enter God's house. But modesty is just the start.

In addition to modest, your church clothing should be appropriate. Your favorite university sweat suit covers you up just fine, but does not qualify as appropriate church clothing. Finally, in addition to modest and appropriate, let me put in a pitch for elegance in church dress. If meeting our Blessed Lord in His sacramental presence is the source and summit of our lives, we should dress the part. When I was a child, everyone dressed beautifully for church, but in recent years, we Americans have turned casual dress into an art form. The better your children are dressed, the better your chances they will behave at Holy Mass.

Unfair, but True

Many of us have seen an awful lot of poorly behaved children in recent years, in parks and playgrounds, restaurants, and shops. When people comment about these public displays, you may hear it blamed on their parents, but rarely on their public, private, or Catholic schools. Sadly, that is not the case with homeschooling. When homeschooled children do not know how to conduct themselves in public spaces, it can reflect badly on the movement. This is especially true in communities where parents have removed their children from the parish school. On the other hand, when your fellow parishioners witness your children being reverent at Mass, it demonstrates to them that concerned parents, teaching at home, raise terrific kids.

Chapter 6

Avoid Overindulgence

With the exception of the imperial offspring of the Ming dynasty and the dauphins of pre-Revolutionary France, contemporary American kids may represent the most indulged young people in the history of the world.

\- Elizabeth Kolbert in *New Yorker* Magazine

An Illinois native planned to move to her husband's native Africa at some point in the future, to raise any children they might have. This news started a lively conversation around our dinner table. "Why," we asked, "would you consider raising children in Africa with all the civil unrest and rampant disease on that continent?" Her answer went right to the point.

"I never saw an African child cry who was not in pain."

Just compare that experience with the whining, crying, complaining, back-talking brats that we all see in church, at the grocery store, and on the playground. Middle-class American children, who enjoy better health, the benefits of a peaceful society, and more material comfort than any children in the history of the world, often seem miserable. According to my friend and others who have lived there, African children laugh and play the day away and are grateful for the tiniest favor, despite often living in what we might describe as grinding poverty. How can this be? When we seek to make our children happy by giving them material things that they demand, are we unwittingly teaching them to be self-centered, greedy, and dissatisfied? The evidence confirms the Biblical admonition that we should not store up for ourselves the world's treasures, nor apparently should we give them to our children.

You may think this is just the observation of a cranky Catholic mother of twelve yearning for the good old days, but the modern secular world is troubled by the behavior of over-indulged children as well. Some time ago, I spotted a brochure advertising a professional workshop for teachers, social workers, and other childcare workers claiming:

> Overindulgence of children has become a serious issue leading children and teens to conduct disorder symptoms. Overindulged children are creating complex community problems, complications for educators and are clogging our legal system.

> The results of parents denying their children nothing are not pretty and have now reached clinical levels.

> The complications of overindulging children include symptoms of conduct disorder, acute self-centeredness, intense detachment leading to anger and resentment fueling misbehavior, excessive dependency, "its-all-about-me"

entitlement, manipulation, loss of self-esteem, missing social skills and impulsiveness.

If a secular organization, which serves daycare workers and public school professionals, is alarmed about the level of selfishness in our young people, we faithful Catholic parents should be frantic. We will remain calm, however, if we keep some simple ideas in mind. A few easy-to-implement tips will go a long way in guarding against overindulgence.

Do not allow children to demand certain clothing.

Preschool teachers report that toddlers, especially girls, are concerned about fashion and very aware of what others think about what they are wearing. We homeschooling moms escape some of this because we limit the amount of time our children spend outside the home, but most of us do not completely escape the effects of TV advertising and peer pressure. Moms of three- and four-year-old daughters report that they often change clothes half a dozen times during the day, leaving discarded garments on the floor. Some boys apparently will insist on wearing super hero costumes for days at a time. This practice must be nipped in the bud for at least five reasons.

First, it makes extra work for mom. Second, with the exception of "Sunday best," preschool children should be so busy playing and learning that they are oblivious to the clothes on their backs. Third, it encourages a "princess (or superhero) syndrome" where little children look cute to get attention, instead of behaving well. This can easily lead to the idea that what is on the outside is more important than what is on the inside. Fourth, it encourages an unchristian attachment to material things. Finally, although it seems pretty harmless, changing clothing often and demanding to wear certain outfits is an example of a child exerting his or her will over that of the parent. Think bridezilla-in-training!

Get in the habit of laying out appropriate clothing before bedtime. Deal with objections in a matter-of-fact manner. "We do not wear our Easter dress to the playground. Tomorrow you are wearing play clothes." Give one warning about changing outfits without permission. If the warning is ignored, box up the clothes and put them out of reach.

Maintain control over the toy box.

American children have way too many toys, and, because they know they will be replaced upon demand, they do not take very good care of them. Some children become selfish with their toys and refuse to allow others to play with them. One mom of a large family allowed her son to mark his toys with black tape so the other children would know not to touch them.

This type of materialism teaches children, at an early age, to be selfish and to value possessions over people. A few simple ideas will help children develop a generous spirit about their belongings.

First, go through the immense pile of toys that most American households accumulate. Toss the broken ones and box the forgotten ones to be given to charity. Ask the child to suggest which playthings should be given away. If the children objects, explain, "You have so many toys you never play with. We are going to give them to children who do not have any toys." Be firm.

Find a shelf or bin for the remaining items. Make sure the children return them to the place they belong after playtime. Try to buy toys that encourage cooperative playtime, like legos, blocks, sidewalk chalk, and simple board games. Often preschool children will go through an age where they become attached to certain toys, like boys with their "army guys" or girls with their kitchen sets. There is nothing wrong with that as long as they are willing to share with others. If children resist sharing, playtime ends. Do that a couple of times, and the nonsense will become very rare indeed.

Do not buy your children something every time you shop.

An hour and a half grocery shopping can be really boring for a child, and there is nothing wrong with buying a bag of pretzels or raisins to occupy them while you shop. I would sometimes bring small hand-held toys or books for the same reason. Occasionally, I would even buy the children some small treat as a reward for especially good behavior. All of these practices are common and not particularly troublesome. The key is to know when a parent crosses the line from being generous to spoiling the child.

There are three signs that might tip you off that your kindness could be eroding your child's character. First, if you buy something for the child every time you go into a shop—even as a reward—that is too much. Children must learn to obey God and their parents, not to receive some small treat or trinket, but because it is the right thing to do. A second sign is if your children ask for something every time you take them shopping. That's a really bad habit! Finally, the most obvious way to tell if you have an overindulged child, is how he or she accepts "no" for an answer. If they scream, cry, or throw a tantrum, you need to take a serious break from buying them anything at all.

As time goes by, let them learn the pitfalls of indulgence themselves.

In modern America, even homeschooled children from the very best families are not immune to the seduction of material things. Although their parents may guard against modern culture, pre-teens and teens often feel deprived if they lack luxuries their friends have, like a Smartphone, a designer handbag, pricey jeans, or high-end sneakers. Now is the time to put all of this in perspective by encouraging personal responsibility and a Catholic outlook about material things.

The most important thing is for parents to simply refuse to give in to demands for these high-priced items. Stand firm! Try to put these requests in perspective so your children realize the logic of your refusal.

"Jane, I simply cannot justify spending $200 for a designer purse when children are starving to death in Third World countries. If I have that kind of money to spare, it is going to charity."

"Bill, we really have to watch our pennies just to pay the bills. We cannot justify spending $125 on sneakers when you can get a perfectly fine pair for a quarter of that price."

Experience is the best teacher, but an expensive one.

I have found that children develop thrifty habits best when they are spending their own hard-earned cash. When my children were pre-teens I announced that I would provide them with the same discount-store clothing that I buy for myself. If they wanted anything more upscale than that, they were welcome to purchase it with their own money.

Some of my children were perfectly satisfied with this arrangement and happily shopped the sale rack. Others worked hard to earn money so they could purchase expensive clothing and electronics. These children learned the value of a buck—or a hundred of them—pretty quickly. Most reformed their ways with no prompting at all from Mom. The essential point is that Mom and Dad have to stand firm and not provide money to replace dollars wasted on frivolous purchases. The kids have to feel the pinch when they cannot go to the movies with their friends because they blew their babysitting money on silly purchases.

Reward your children for good behavior with your praise. Help them develop appropriate Christian attitudes about their toys and clothing. Let them realize that earthly happiness comes from time spent with those we love, not material things.

Chapter 7

A Servant Heart

Now we hear that there are some among you who are living in idleness, doing no work themselves but interfering with everyone else's. In the Lord Jesus Christ we order and call on people of this kind to go on quietly working and earning the food they eat. My brothers and sisters, never grow tired of doing what is right.

- 2 Thessalonians: 11-13

The greatest virtues are those which are most useful to other persons.

- Aristotle

An article in the July 2, 2012 edition of *New Yorker* magazine created quite a stir among American parents and gives Catholic homeschooling moms and dads a reason to examine their own family lives. A sociologist, studying a tribe of indigenous people in South America, accompanied one family on a trip into the jungle to gather leaves. A member of another family, Yanira, went along and, without being asked, made herself useful by sweeping the sleeping mats and stacking the collected leaves. Later in the day, Yanira would fish, and then clean and cook her catch for the entire group. The sociologist was very impressed by the calm and self-possessed Yanira, most especially because she was only six years old. That's right, six years old!

In the urban area where I live, I often see children of that age still being pushed in strollers because their parents don't want to listen to them whine if they force them to walk. They are unable to tie their own shoelaces, and are not even sure which shoe goes on which foot. They have no regular chores, and have to be begged and cajoled into performing even the simplest tasks. At first grade age, they are not ashamed to cry when they do not get their own way. Even in large homeschooling families, where the children are more cooperative and competent, I certainly do not see any of them fixing supper. Where are we going wrong and what can we do about it?

Train them up in the way they should go

Before they enter the first grade, every child should be solely responsible for a number of regular chores. They should be making their beds and stowing their pajamas under the pillow and their clean laundry in drawers and closets. They should put their dirty clothing in the hamper and tidy their own rooms. In addition to cleaning up their own messes, they should help set and clear the table for meals and share in the care of younger siblings. Perhaps most importantly, they should keep their workspaces in order, and start their schoolwork on time without being told.

In the primary grades 1st through 3rd, your students will learn the basics of reading, 'riting, 'rithmetic, and in our Catholic homeschools, religion as well. At the same time, and in much the same way, they should be learning all the basics of homemaking. At this age children can be taught to fold laundry, commencing with towels and washcloths and graduating to apparel, and then distributing it to the appropriate destinations. Jobs necessitating the use of large muscles—vacuuming, sweeping, and raking—are ideal to burn off some of the excess energy primary age students exhibit.

During the middle school years, your children should be trained, at Mom and Dad's side, in all the skills needed to run a thrifty, tidy home. Let them shop for food with you, chop greens for salads while you mix the dressing, and follow a recipe to bake cookies for dessert. When they are old enough and sufficiently responsible, teach each child how safely and properly to clean each room in your house by demonstrating how you mend, dust, mop, scrub the tiles around the tub, and wash dishes. Teach them how to sort wash and operate the washer and dryer. When a child is old enough and mature enough to obey safety instructions, turn over lawn mowing duties.

Assigning Chores

Some parents rotate chores among the children, assigning kitchen duty on particular nights, or posting a job schedule on the refrigerator. I have found, on the contrary, that allowing children to assume long-term responsibilities gives them a proprietary feeling, and they take greater pride in a job well done. For example, if your nine-year-old loves to bake, put her in charge of desserts. She might really enjoy moving beyond packaged mixes and looking for simple recipes to add to her repertoire. Accept her requests for ingredients that must be added to the shopping list. It's her job; let her do it.

In our house, one daughter had the responsibility of keeping the much-used upstairs bathroom clean for her high school years. In this case, familiarity led to a high level of cleanliness! Because this was "her" room, she scolded anyone who failed to rinse the tub or put away the toothpaste. When another daughter cleans the kitchen, she is fast to direct late-night snackers to put their dishes in the sink. Children are more cooperative about keeping the house tidy when they feel a sense of ownership.

Training your children in housekeeping has many benefits. The less time you have to spend on household tasks, the more time you have to teach lessons. As children become skillful and competent around the house, they gain confidence and true self-esteem from a job well done. Additionally, performing chores around the house helps your children grow in the virtue of industriousness. Developing habits of hard work will serve them well throughout their lifetimes, and will help them resist one of the sins against the theological virtue of hope: despair. When the going gets tough, industrious people roll up their sleeves and tackle whatever comes their way.

Serving Others

If your children are doing their chores on a regular basis without too much complaining, now is the time to give them the gift of a servant heart. A Christian does not "find himself" through self-reflection, rather he finds his true calling in service to others. Parents teach heroic service by word and example. At least part of your homeschool reading assignments should concentrate on the lives of saints, especially those like St. Zita, Blessed Teresa of Calcutta, St. John Vianney, St. Frances Xavier Cabrini, and others who lived busy, industrious lives.

Parish Confirmation preparation classes often insist that the confirmandi volunteer some hours to a homeless shelter or soup kitchen. My daughter Beth repaired houses for people in Appalachia through a parish-sponsored program. Even young children can fill baby bottles with change to raise money for crisis pregnancy centers. All of these are worthy efforts, but our earliest and most regular opportunities for service start a lot closer to home.

You can give great example to your children so they get in the habit of looking to serve others they meet. Here are some ideas:

- In the car, wave on pedestrians, even if you have the right of way.
- Let the person with just a few items behind you in the checkout line go before your overflowing big family cart.
- Return bikes and scooters that the neighbors' children leave strewn all over the neighborhood.

- Offer to drive elderly neighbors to church or shopping.
- Drop off meals to homes dealing with difficult situations.
- Take an hour and help a neighbor clean house or yard.

Frequently suggest opportunities for service to your children. If you are going grocery shopping, ask the children to run to an elderly neighbor's home, to see if you can pick something up. Suggest your child shovel snow or rake leaves for a neighbor who might have trouble doing it himself – and not for pay. Perhaps they can offer to walk a dog on an icy day. Today, with extended families so scattered, there are lots of openings to help young parents struggling with multiple toddlers. Your children can carry groceries. Perhaps a teen can offer to sit outside and keep an eye on playing children, so Mom has a chance to start supper. Service to others becomes a habit when we look for opportunities.

The ability to work hard becomes a habit. If your children are useful around your house and community, these good habits will spill over into other areas of their lives, like their homeschooling. Those who are generally industrious are far more likely to be motivated when faced with academic challenges. They gain confidence in their own abilities when they master new tasks. Never forget that we Catholics believe that they will also get actual graces for all the good acts they perform, and these graces in turn will help then accomplish even greater deeds. Start insisting that your children work by your side today.

Chapter 8

Homeschooling with Virtue

The power of man's virtue should not be measured by his special efforts, but by his ordinary doing.

- Blaise Pascal

In the 1984 film, *The Karate Kid*, Mr. Miyagi promises to teach martial arts to Daniel, the bullied son of a single mother. When Daniel shows up for his first lesson, he expects to learn kicks and blocks. Instead Mr. Miyagi instructs him to wax the car, sand a floor, refinish a fence, and paint the house using specific motions—like a counter-clockwise rotation of the hand. Daniel is frustrated, believing he has learned nothing about karate, but Mr. Miyagi finally explains that the young man has actually been putting defensive blocks into his "muscle memory" with these repetitive movements. Daniel achieves blackbelt karate skills by first mastering the basic essentials at a far less exciting level.

When are we going to talk about homeschooling?

You finished a good portion of this book and may have noticed that very little time has been devoted to actual homeschooling. It might seem odd for a book written with homeschooling fathers and mothers in mind, but like Mr. Miyagi, I have been passing along necessary elements of home education. When virtues like patience, order, obedience, and courtesy are in the "muscle memory" of your family's life, homeschooling is not only possible, it becomes a joy.

Homeschoolers face diverse challenges. Perhaps some of you are just embarking on your homeschool journey. Others worry that their progress will slam to a halt with the birth of another baby. Some experienced homeschooling parents are intimidated by the demands of high school subjects like algebra, chemistry, and foreign language. In our Catholic homes, many moms simply feel overwhelmed by the sheer number of children and the volume of material that must be presented. It does not matter what the needs of your individual situation, the solution is always the same. The basic essentials of calm, confident, consistent parenting, which produces cooperative, competent children, will get you through any difficulties that arise.

The Home School of Virtue

This little book has already presented these essentials to you by asking you to raise virtuous children, children who respond confidently, obediently, even eagerly, to the demands of whatever environment in which the family finds itself. When you exercise your God-given authority over them from their earliest years, your children learn *obedience* as required by the Fourth Commandment. Attentive participation at Mass teaches *reverence* and *respect*. By discouraging constant snacking while encouraging good eating habits, you teach *moderation* and *restraint*. Consistent and reliable meal and sleep schedules teach your children *patience* and *serenity*. By insisting on good manners in your home, your children learn *cheerfulness, selflessness,* and *courtesy.* Your children learn *generosity* and *detachment from material things* when they do not have every whim indulged. When they pitch in and help with household chores, you inculcate habits of *responsibility, industriousness,* and *resourcefulness.* Most importantly, from constant affectionate interaction with parents, siblings, grandparents, and extended family members, children absorb the theological virtue of *charity* – Christian love.

Homeschooling with Virtue

Let's see how all this works in practice during a typical, although mythical, homeschooling day in a busy Catholic household based on my own experience. Mom Marie and Dad Anthony have four children: Angela is in the 3rd grade, Benedict is in the 1st, 4-year-old Catherine is in pre-K, and baby Dennis is 2. Marie is expecting another baby in a couple of months, so her energy level is not too high. Because she has trouble getting out of bed in the morning, Mom makes sure the children lay out their clothing before they go to bed at night. Everyone wakes up at 7:00, and the three oldest children get themselves dressed while Marie helps Dennis. When she goes to the kitchen to prepare breakfast, Angela and Benedict stow everyone's PJ's and make their own beds.

The children eat breakfast at 7:30, and the three oldest help to clear the dishes.

At 8 A.M., the two oldest start schoolwork. Angela has a desk in the corner of the living room where she works off a list in her lesson planner. She can usually finish penmanship, phonics, spelling, vocabulary, and math on her own. If she does not understand a concept, she pushes that book to the side and starts on another. Benedict cannot do much schoolwork on his own yet, but he can start penmanship while Mom finishes the breakfast dishes. Mom brings Catherine and Dennis into the playroom and tells them to play with the toy kitchen set. She will work with Benedict for about forty minutes until the little children begin to interrupt. Then she sends Benedict in to play with Dennis, and does a few pages in the pre-K books with Catherine.

At 10 A.M., everyone takes a 15-minute snack break. Later, Angela plays with the two youngest children while Mom works with Benedict, and then the two oldest children swap roles, and Mom reviews the work that Angela began on her own. Everyone breaks for lunch at noon, and immediately after, Dennis goes down for a nap and Catherine lies on her bed where she can watch a saint biography video for "quiet time."

During naptime, Mom reads with Benedict and helps Angela with her English. As all the religion books cover the same material in the same order, she reads the third grade religion lesson out loud to both children. She reviews the grade level questions and answers with each child. The children share history and science lessons. Both children are finished with their schoolwork before naptime is over and, after helping to tidy up the house, go outside to play.

Seems too easy!

The reason all this works for our mythical mom Marie is because she worked hard inculcating the virtues in her children practically from birth. Angela can do schoolwork on her own because she has helped around the house for as long as she can remember. She can wait for her mom's help with assignments because she has learned patience waiting for meals, and she knows it is rude to interrupt. Angela and Benedict know what is expected of them at any particular time because they are accustomed to a regular and predictable schedule of sleeping, waking, eating, schoolwork, chores, prayer, and play. They are attentive at home just as they are in church. The children are generally kind and cooperative with one another, especially with the baby, because they have been raised with Christian charity, in a household where polite manners are the rule, and not reserved for special occasions.

Does this really work?

Mostly. My own homeschooling operated like this for many years. Glitches occurred when circumstances forced us to depart from our schedule. I had an infant and a toddler when I started homeschooling five older children my first year. One moment everything was humming along nicely, and the next minute school was suspended as Mom raced the two-year-old to the hospital for stitches. Stomach bugs, a fridge on the fritz, a visit from grandma, all of these things can really upset even the smoothest of schedules. But the whole family can remain calm because they work together as a team. Problems arrive, and they get solved in time.

On the other hand, when the kids are out of control, the unavoidable issues that every family encounters are compounded. Homeschooling is virtually impossible if it is a daily struggle to get the children into bed at night or out of it the next morning, and children bolt to the TV every time Mom's back is turned. I am serious when I maintain that homeschooling needs to take place in a home with strong faith, consistent rules and scheduling, and children who are generally obedient and cooperative. Effective discipline is the key to successful home education.

Chapter 9

Is It Too Late for Us?

The key of persistence opens all doors closed by resistance.

- John Di Lemme

I have been talking about the important role discipline plays in Catholic home education for over twenty years. After my talks, almost without fail, a couple of parents will pull me to the side to ask a "personal question." The question is always the same. "We wish we had heard you years ago, when our children were younger. We rarely corrected them and made it a point to praise everything they did to build self-esteem. We allowed them to argue with us and tried to reason with them. Now at 10 and 12, they are entitled tyrants. They give us a hard time about everything. We pulled them out of school because the teachers said they needed to be medicated for ADHD, but they are impossible to homeschool. They may have to go back. In just a few short years, they will be teens. What then? Is it too late for us?" The answers to these questions are something like the old joke: there is good news and bad news.

The Good News

The goodness of God and our own human experience teach us that there is always hope. Many parents report that their children, while terribly misbehaved at home, do obey their teachers in school or the coaches in organized sports, proving they are capable of controlling themselves. Boarding schools and sleep-away camps, which specialize in therapeutic care for troubled youth, often report great success by implementing many of the same techniques recommended here. I was a foster mother for fifteen years, and I can tell you that many very troubled children from the worst possible home situations were capable of profound change in a loving Catholic environment. We need never give up on our children; with God's grace, there is always hope.

The Bad News

If you have not exercised your God-given authority right from the start, you may be stuck with a transformation that will take quite some time. Be patient with yourselves and with your children. True change is possible, but it is tough. Here are some ideas for you to think about.

First Things First

Tell your children, "You are required by the Fourth Commandment of God to love, honor, and respect your mother and your father. You have failed on numerous occasions, so we are going to Confession so you can confess these sins against the Fourth Commandment, and be forgiven."

But do not stop there. "We, your parents, should have insisted that you learn and obey the Fourth Commandment.

As we have not done this, we are going to Confession too. Then we are all going to have a firm intention not to commit these sins again."

Clean up the Environment

If your children are still in institutional schools, now is the time to pull them out. New homeschooling parents need to remember that the first months of home education may not be very productive from an academic standpoint. Often children need months to "detox" from the anti-Christian, anti-authority, crass and vulgar culture of too many American schools. Gradually introduce Catholic practices, prayer, daily Mass when possible, the family Rosary, and frequent Confession. Remember: change takes time.

Do Not Argue with Your Children

You have allowed your children to argue with you, and responded by trying to reason with them. It hasn't worked. Just stop it. If, for example, your son wants to go somewhere with his friends, and you do not think it is a good idea, just say no. If he argues with you, cut him short. "I am not going to change my mind, so there is no sense in your arguing with me."

Now if you have allowed your children to yell at you in the past or be otherwise disrespectful, he might start to holler or say nasty things, and you would have the understandable desire to yell back, "Don't you speak to me that way!"

Remember that the only reason your son is yelling at you is because you have tolerated this in the past. Accept his bad behavior as a penance for your past sins, and walk away. Refuse to engage him. "I am not listening to you when you speak disrespectfully." Later, when you and he have calmed down, you may add a punishment, "You are certainly not going to watch TV tonight after the way you spoke to me this afternoon," or you simply may discuss his behavior. Make it straightforward. "Do not ever raise your voice to me. I expect an apology."

Eliminate Electronics

Often parents will ask me what consequences they should give their children for bad behavior. It is not a good idea to threaten your children with particular punishments. There is always the danger that you will not follow through. In the heat of anger, parents sometimes inflict ridiculous punishments ("You are grounded until Christmas!") which are worse than nothing at all. In large families, who can keep track of punishments?

A better way is to simply express your displeasure, "I am very disappointed that you would say such a thing." Wait and then, presuming you remember, inflict a consequence—no dessert or no TV tonight. "This will help you remember not to speak to me like you did this afternoon."

I am a big fan of eliminating electronics. There is a mountain of evidence that tells us that "screen time" is not good for children. (Seeing kids playing video games in restaurants is a pet peeve of mine. Why can't they participate in the conversation?) TV is especially toxic for children with behavioral issues. Too many programs feature rude, know-it-all kids, and ineffective, stupid parents. Video games are often violent and anti-social. Screen time should be severely limited or eliminated entirely, thus providing you with a perfect punishment for misbehavior.

Be Ready to Take Tough Action

Parents have told me that they have taken away video games as a punishment, and the kids retrieve them out of the closet when Mom's back is turned. There is only one response to that: throw the games out! It doesn't matter that this was Grandma's gift last Christmas; the kids have to know that you mean business.

If you catch the children watching TV during school time, unplug it and put it into the basement. If you catch them trying to retrieve it, cancel the cable and have dad bring the set to his workplace. Often it's the parents who do not want to live without the TV. Too bad! This is the price you will have to pay to get your kids in line.

The same principle applies in public places. If the children are unruly in a restaurant, or argue at an amusement park, give them one warning, then follow through and leave. Don't let them promise to be better, then renege, then promise again. One warning; if behavior does not change, you go home. Never mind that you already paid for your food or for admission. Accept any monetary loss as a penance for your failure to raise cooperative kids and then deduct it from their allowances. You will only have to do this once or twice before the kids know you will follow through.

Allow Them to Make Up for Bad Behavior

Remember, they are children. If they have behaved badly, but seem to be trying to make up for it, forgive them and move on. (That's another reason I am not a fan of long-term consequences.) Some children apologize; accept it. Others have difficulty verbalizing, but will be especially cooperative or do an extra chore. Always respond positively to these types of overtures. It is just as important, perhaps more important, to reinforce good behaviors as to correct bad ones.

Seek Professional Help

Bad behavior, resulting from ineffective parenting, is too often labeled "conduct disorder" and treated with medication, instead of parents and children taking responsibility and making changes. Nevertheless, there are some children who suffer from diagnosable clinical behavioral disorders. If many months of consistent, calm correction have not yielded any results, it might be time for a professional evaluation.

I urge you, if possible, to locate a Catholic professional, or at least one who will be respectful of Catholic values. Your parish priest or diocesan office may be of assistance to you here. Often childcare professionals will recommend many of the techniques in this book: a reliable schedule, insistence on a respectful environment, regular chores, and others, but some children need more.

A word of warning is in order. Some behavioral specialists recommend sending the child to public school for "therapeutic services." This may be necessary in a handful of cases where the child's continued presence in the home is creating a hostile situation for the other children, but it should only be a last resort.

Pray! Pray! Pray!

St. Monica prayed for her son for decades while he lived a life of unrepentant dissipation. Finally, she was granted the grace to see his conversion in his middle years. Although she died before Augustine became a priest, bishop, and great teacher of the Church, she enjoyed tremendous peace and joy. Here are her final words as recorded by her son, St. Augustine of Hippo:

> Son, for myself, I have no longer any pleasure in anything in this life. What I want here further, and why I am here, I know not, now that my hopes in this world are satisfied. There was indeed one thing for which I wished to tarry a little in this life, and that was that I might see you a Catholic Christian before I died. My God has exceeded this abundantly, so that I see you despising all earthly felicity, made His servant—what do I here? (*Confessions* IX, 10)

Entrust your family to the intercession of St. Monica. Pray, pray for God's blessings on the important task of raising your children to be adults who are ready to lead Catholics in the next generation.

Chapter 10

Some Final Points to Ponder

Thus the home is the first school of Christian life, and "a school for human enrichment." Here one learns endurance and the joy of work, fraternal love, generous – even repeated – forgiveness, and above all divine worship in prayer and the offering of one's life.

- CCC §1657

My hope is that this little book is useful to you and gives you a few simple tools that you can use to establish your God-given authority over your children, so that they grow in virtue. Primarily, I want you to accept the fact that God has given you these children, not just to love them, as I am sure you do, but also to form their character. Right before the vows in a Catholic wedding, the priest asks the couple, "Will you accept children lovingly from God, and *bring them up according to the law of Christ and His Church*?" *The Catechism of the Catholic Church* tells us, "Parents are the principle and first *educators* of their children" (§1653). (Emphasis is mine in both quotes.) These holy sources presume your affection for your children, so they emphasize your duty to raise them well.

Although like many of you, I began homeschooling to protect my children from the noxious environment of institutional schools and to provide a more rigorous academic setting, these cannot be our primary motivations. Our first goal as parents must be to prepare our children for eternal salvation, by giving them a love and understanding of Catholic principles – in other words, to teach them to be saints.

Just do it! Homeschool!

For over twenty years, I have been encouraging parents to put aside their doubts and fears and teach their children at home. At first, many of these parents struggle with their children's poor behavior, caused both by lax parenting and the anti-authority environment in many institutional schools. The simple action of home education often has a positive effect on your children's conduct, perhaps because they are no longer influenced by rude, disobedient classmates. It might be because Mom and Dad can no longer ignore misbehavior by shipping the kids off to school. Whatever the reason, outsiders are often flabbergasted by polite, well-behaved homeschooled children who exhibit a maturity well beyond their years.

There are some very fine, high-quality Catholic schools, and in a country as immense as the United States, I do not dismiss the possibility that some public schools may provide a very fine environment as well. Nevertheless, experience has clearly shown that loving parents who provide their children with a thoroughly Catholic education, in a home that stresses virtue, will raise up children of noble character and impeccable integrity. Our seminaries and convents are quickly filling up with graduates from the "school of the home." Teach your children at home.

Don't forget Dad!

For some reason, no matter how tough a disciplinarian a woman may be, children just listen better to a strong father. I used to joke that once my sons began to shave, I could tie them to a tree and flog them and they would just yawn in my face. If my husband told them to jump, they said, "Yes, Sir! How high?" There is just something about dads!

Dad, as soon as you get home from work, ask Mom how the children behaved that day. Often just knowing Mom is giving you a report will keep a mischievous child in check. If little Johnny is a particular problem, give him more individual attention. Before you go to work in the morning, explain to Johnny just what your expectations are regarding his behavior during the day. Be very clear. "Don't let your mother tell me that you gave her a hard time today. I'm going to be asking her when I get home." If you usually go to work before the children get out of bed, no problem. Wake Johnny up! He'll know you mean business.

If you find some time, call home during your lunch. Cut right to the chase. "Let me speak to Johnny. Son, do you remember what I said before I left for work today? I do! Make sure you are listening to your mother today." Often, a big dose of Dad is just the remedy for a tough kid.

Idle hands are the devil's workshop.

Possibly the worst habit of modern children is "hanging out." First of all, there is no such thing. Kids with nothing to do will find something to do, often something of which parents do not approve. Sometimes that means time in front of a TV or computer screen. Keep your children busy with wholesome activities.

Life in the typical homeschooling family provides plenty of opportunities to stay busy, like schoolwork, household chores, babysitting younger siblings, and family devotions. School age children, though, have an awful lot of energy, and lots of time on their hands. If at all possible, try to set up an outside space so the kids can get plenty of fresh air and sunshine. In the early years, do not be too concerned if you do not have the time or money to get your children into organized sports or other activities. Generations of young people grew up playing in the backyard with their siblings and neighbors and turned out just fine. In addition, unorganized play helps children become more self-reliant. I have noticed that one good consequence of all these families with just one or two kids is how easy it is to buy used toys for next to nothing. Insist that your younger children get several hours of free play, outside if possible, most days.

As children get older, there can be a place for organized sports and other activities, like music, scouting, or debating. Many thrive in the disciplined environment of advanced level competitive or group activities. They are forced to put forth their best efforts and learn the valuable lesson that, sometimes, despite one's best efforts, a person may still fall short of a goal. For American children, who are often spared even the tiniest bit of disappointment, this may be the only place they gain this experience. An intense outside activity often requires that children acquire and use an advanced skill set. They need to be on time for practices and classes, listen carefully to instructions, and often study or practice on their own. Then, they will perform or otherwise showcase this skill in front of others. In my own mega-family, the children had to help pay for their activities as well. All of these actions can lead to greater virtue and maturity.

Many localities are blessed with Catholic homeschool support groups, which offer a wide range of activities. When there are no organized homeschool activities nearby, concerned parents worry—with some justification—that extracurricular activities will expose their children to unwholesome environments. Of course, parents are wise to consider each situation in its context and investigate. (For example, I have some strong reservations about the Girl Scouts at the national level.) We need to remember, however, that few outside endeavors are as wholesome as the controlled environment of a Catholic home. By discussing what goes on in the world with our children, we can turn what they are discovering about American culture into a learning experience, and introduce them to discernment.

If you remember nothing else...

Remember this! Your homeschooling will only be successful—may only be possible—if you raise virtuous children who can be counted on to do what they are supposed to do. Much the same can be said about the chance for happy family life, your children's later academic and professional pursuits, and the honor and character of these future citizens of the United States. More than ever before, our country needs leaders of the strongest ability and integrity in every area of professional endeavor. The United States needs men and women to excel in the fields of medicine, politics, journalism, commerce, and the law. The Catholic Church needs men and women to enter the priesthood and religious life, and well-formed laymen to bring the gospel of Jesus Christ into secular society.

None of this is easy in our present culture. Parents have been marginalized, and parenting articles on the Internet have replaced traditional wisdom and plain old common sense. Your children's playmates and teammates are often overindulged and rude. Moms are rarely home in most neighborhoods, and as this book is being written, tough economic times have forced men to work longer hours, making Mom's job solitary—even lonely—and Dad more exhausted than ever. No matter, you must persevere.

Pray in front of the Blessed Sacrament. Beg the intercession of Mary, the Mother of God, and of the saints. Pray to your children's guardian angels, and your own. With God's grace, all things are possible.